HINDEMITH

Oxford Studies of Composers

General Editor : Colin Mason

Egon Wellesz: FUX
Denis Arnold: MARENZIO
Basil Deane: CHERUBINI
Paul Doe: TALLIS
Anthony Payne: SCHOENBERG
Jerome Roche: PALESTRINA
Norman Kay: SHOSTAKOVICH
Gilbert Reaney: MACHAUT

Oxford Studies of Composers (6)

HINDEMITH

IAN KEMP

London
OXFORD UNIVERSITY PRESS

Oxford University Press, Ely House, London W.1

GLASGOW   NEW YORK   TORONTO   MELBOURNE   WELLINGTON
CAPE TOWN   IBADAN   NAIROBI   DAR ES SALAAM   LUSAKA   ADDIS ABABA
DELHI   BOMBAY   CALCUTTA   MADRAS   KARACHI   LAHORE   DACCA
KUALA LUMPUR   SINGAPORE   HONG KONG   TOKYO

ISBN 0 19 314118 3

© Oxford University Press 1970

*Printed in Great Britain
by W & J Mackay Limited
Chatham, Kent*

ACKNOWLEDGEMENTS

I WOULD like to record my gratitude to the late Mrs. Gertrude Hindemith and to David Drew and Hugh Wood for help and advice on a number of points, to the University of Aberdeen for financial assistance, and to B. Schotts Söhne, Mainz and Schott and Co. Ltd., London for the loan of music and access to their archives. All music examples are reprinted by kind permission of B. Schotts Söhne, Mainz.

In memory of my father
22 xi 63

DEVELOPMENTS TOWARDS
NEO-CLASSICISM

AFTER the 1914–18 war Germany needed a new composer. Reger had died in 1916, and neither Strauss nor Pfitzner were advocates of the New Music. An eager audience was waiting to acclaim their successor. Hindemith was fortunate in finding a platform as well as an audience ready for him. The Donaueschingen Festival, which was destined to play an influential role in the history of contemporary music, was founded precisely when his creative talent was becoming really individual. The success of his Quartet no. 2 at the first festival of 1921 and the furore which greeted his *Kammermusik nr. 1* at the second quickly established his position as leader of Germany's avant-garde composers.

For this second festival he wrote the following little autobiography:

I was born in Hanau in 1895. Music study from the age of twelve. As violinist, violist, pianist or percussionist I have made a thorough survey of the following musical territories: chamber music of all kinds, cinema, café, dance music, operetta, jazz band, military music. I have been leader of the Frankfurt Opera Orchestra since 1916. As composer, I have chiefly written pieces I don't like any more: chamber music for the most diverse ensembles, songs and piano pieces. Also three one-act operas, which will probably remain the only ones since as a result of rising prices on the manuscript paper market only small scores can now be written.

I cannot give analyses of my works because I don't know how to explain a piece of music in a few words (I would rather write a new one in the time). Besides I think that for people with ears my things are perfectly easy to understand, so an analysis is superfluous. For people without ears such cribs can't help. Neither do I write out single themes, which always give a false impression.

The facts of his early career speak for themselves; they are remarkable enough. Perhaps, however, one should add that he was born on 16 November 1895, that Hanau is near Frankfurt am Main (where he was to live until 1927), that his 'music study' was at the Hoch Conservatory, Frankfurt, and that his extra-mural activities were undertaken, against the wishes of his teachers, to augment his family income. He might also have mentioned that he was the founder and viola player of the Amar Quartet,[1] even if he did not then know that it would be recognized so soon as one of the leading quartets in Europe. But a reference to this would doubtless have been laconic: he was not one to draw attention to his personal history. His aim in the autobiography was to dispel the mystique popularly surrounding the creative artist and to reveal himelf as a normal human being with his feet squarely on the ground.

*   *   *

He had to be cajoled into submitting scores for the first festival. But he finally sent a total of seven, providing the festival committee with a clear indication of his remarkable fluency, his predisposition towards chamber music and his progressive idiom. The earliest of them was the Quartet no. 1 in F minor, op. 10 (1918).[2]

Although this work leans heavily on classical models, both stylistic and formal, its assurance of manner and adventurousness in detail show that even in his earliest works Hindemith was intent on renewing the classical tradition of chamber music. The first movement contains the only obvious instance in his published music of the influence of Reger,[3] most explicit in the chromatic fugato which acts as a development section. The second movement leaves Regerish affiliations far behind. It is barely possible to relate the harmony of the theme, for example, to traditional procedure. The attempt to do so (Ex. 1) indicates that it is better looked at in terms of line.

Ex.1

[1] The Havemann Quartet had been engaged to perform the Quartet no. 2, but refused to do so. The Amar Quartet (Licco Amar, Heinrich Kaspar, Hindemith, and—initially—his brother Rudolf, then Maurits Frank) was formed in order that the work could be heard.

[2] Hindemith's second published work (the first was the Three Pieces, op. 8, for cello and piano). It was originally titled Quartet no. 2. An earlier quartet in C, op. 2, was shelved later.

[3] Hindemith's undoubted kinship with Reger is shown in the common interests of polyphony, the revival of baroque forms, the emphasis on compositional techniques. In this respect Reger's influence is deep and lasting, providing an important link in the chain which connects Hindemith with his great German predecessors. When, during the latter part of his life, Hindemith became increasingly active as a conductor, Reger's music was prominent in his programmes. He made an edition of Reger's 100*th Psalm* for chorus and orchestra in 1958.

The five string sonatas of op. 11 concentrate particularly on this type of linear chromaticism. The vehemently energetic cello sonata, no. 3 of the opus (1919), is notably free from traditional harmonic thinking. Many passages in no. 5, a solo viola sonata, are almost atonal, the music being held together by strong semitonal connections no less advanced for their indebtedness to the *Tristan* principle of semitonal movement. The most substantial work in the group, the sonata for viola and piano, (no. 4) is still conceived harmonically, deriving now from Strauss, now from Debussy, now from a variety of other influences. This, however, does not obscure the work's inventive qualities nor its originality in the formal sphere: an introduction is followed by a theme and first set of variations which build up to the finale, a second set of variations.

The feverishly expressionistic atmosphere of the first movement of the Quartet no. 2, op. 16 (1921), proclaims a debt here to Schoenberg, and in particular to the melodic gestures of the latter's Chamber Symphony. The wide span of the opening theme, the major-minor chords, unresolved appoggiaturas, fourth-cords (all given direction by semitonal movement)—the language is used with conviction.

Ex.2

This and the Tristanesque slow movement mark the limit, in musical terms, of Hindemith's excursion into expressionism. More notorious examples, however, were the one-act operas, which were all first performed at well-known opera houses and which therefore attracted wider journalistic attention than the quartet. They were largely responsible for his early reputation as a provocateur. But their texts, sensational though they are, were typical products of the postwar years and it was only to be expected that Hindemith should feel drawn to Oscar Kokoschka's *Mörder, Hoffnung der Frauen* (Murder, Hope of Women) and August Stramm's *Sancta Susanna*, both of which were first published in an influential avant-garde magazine, *Der Sturm*. Expressionism was a powerful force and Kokoschka and Stramm were major expressionists, providing fashionable texts which Hindemith, without undue reflection, could set to music.

Mörder, Hoffnung der Frauen is an autobiographical and elemental outpouring about sexual conflict. What makes the opera (1919) less than a success is the disparity between the perfunctory music, compounded of Wagner, Puccini, and Strauss, and the obscurity of the text. *Sancta Susanna* is a description of how a young nun is induced by a spring night, a glimpse of peasant love, and an account of sexual ecstasy in another nun to tear her clothes off and embrace the altar crucifix in a frenzy. On a deeper level Stramm makes a plea for understanding of profound urges and instincts. As a theatrical composer Hindemith shows considerable enterprise in the opera (1921). It is tightly controlled dramatically and more integrated stylistically. The very consistency of style, however, focuses attention on the anonymity of its musical language, and the work can be regarded only as a successful exercise.

Das Nusch-Nuschi (1920), designed to be performed by Burmese marionettes, is far more sophisticated than either of the other two. Hindemith demonstrates here that while discovering expressionism he could at the same time poke fun at its musical godfather. The text is by Franz Blei (an editor of several magazines and a translator). It may be judged an after-dinner whimsy, mildly erotic and effecting gentle inroads into the absurd. Half alligator, half rat, the Nusch-Nuschi terrifies the drunken field-marshal, Kyce Waing, who is accused of enjoying the Emperor's four wives. King Mark's words to Tristan (*Tristan und Isolde*, Act 2) are admirably suited to the situation: 'Mir dies!' Hindemith's quotation, though almost exact, is distorted by a persistent wrong note in the bass. The field-marshal's punishment is 'the usual'—castration.

His reputation was given a riotous boost with the first performance of the *Kammermusik nr. 1 mit Finale 1921*, op. 24, no. 1. Its very title debunks cherished ideals (chamber music indeed!); the twelve performers are directed to be invisible to the public (an insult to the concert-goer): the instrumentation includes accordion, trumpet, and percussion (obvious collusion with jazz); the 'brutish' finale accommodates a popular foxtrot of the day, imaginatively titled 'Fuchstanz', by the Berlin cabaret composer Wilm-Wilm (Ex. 3); and the work ends with

Ex.3

a shriek on a siren (collusion here with the noisy Futurists). Hindemith was trespassing on the preserves of Dada. Musically it placed him in a no-man's-land half-way between a Stravinskian aesthetic and empirical experiment. The first movement is undoubtedly the finest *Petrushka*-derivative of the twentieth century. As an instance of deft felony it is unrivalled. Other noteworthy features include a passing flirtation with gamelan sonorities, and a more systematic investigation of polytonal combinations. (Hindemith's most extended use of polytonal harmonies is to be found in the final movement of *Tanzstücke* for piano, op. 19, an attractive occasional piece.)

The dalliance with jazz and the world of the night-club accounted for the composition of the *Suite 1922*, op. 26, for piano, a work which at one time shared the fame of the *Kammermusik*. Its five movements are March, Shimmy, Nocturne, Boston, and Ragtime. It has documentary interest, and can be regarded as a ponderous piece of satire, palliated somewhat by a verbal bonne-bouche at the head of the Ragtime: 'Direction for Use. Pay no attention to what you've learnt at piano lessons. Don't spend a long time considering whether you should play D sharp with the fourth or the sixth finger. Play this piece wildly, but with very strict rhythm. Regard the piano here as an interesting form of percussion and act accordingly.' With the *Suite* Hindemith's interest in jazz was played out, and it was reawakened in later works only by strictly functional demands. But it had served its purpose. Apart from contributing towards the decisive, because deliberate, rejection of expressionism (this is the real significance of the *Kammermusik*), it also confirmed Hindemith's leanings towards the chamber ensemble. This medium may in the first instance have provided merely a convenient outlet for his reaction against the mammoth orchestra of late romanticism (he was, after all, the only major composer who had first-hand experience of playing in Wagner performances); but its use quickly became second nature to him.

If the rather desperate attitudes and wild techniques behind the *Kammermusik nr. 1* reflect Hindemith's unsureness as a composer at that time, the *Kleine Kammermusik* for wind quintet, op. 24, no. 2 (1922), suddenly presents a different picture. In this scintillating little work, the macaronic style is superseded by one of consistency and originality. Self-conscious audacity is transformed into wit. The contrasted timbres of the instruments have acted as a spur to the creation of clear sprightly lines, owing something to the inevitable Frenchness of the medium and rather more to archetypes in the dance tradition of the eighteenth century. The first theme, perfectly adjusted to the proportions and character of the work as a whole, is a model of the type Hindemith was subsequently to make his own: chromatic in general content, but constructed in diatonic units linked melodically by the same principle of overlap that informs the harmonic innovations of previous centuries. The aural demands of this swift melodic modulation are compensated for by familiar rhythmic patterns, which quite naturally release it from harmonic obligations.

Ex.4

The Quartet no. 3, op. 22, of the same year, vividly demonstrates Hindemith's mastery of the medium. Of all his quartets, it contains the most inventive new sounds. But a still powerful residue of expressionist and other influences remains. Thus the first movement, headed 'Fugato', cannot avoid conventional extensions of short-winded espressivo melodic phrases which lead inevitably to an earnest central climax in the Romantic manner. The second movement, with its ostinati and Magyar flourishes, owes a great deal to Bartók, as does the third, where polytonality is used to create piquant and haunting major-minor clashes. The last two movements, however, show greater individuality. The fourth, which involves cadenzas for the cello and viola like the corresponding movement in the *Kleine Kammermusik*, acts as a prelude to the finale, where an opening two-part invention for viola and cello recalls the cool emotional climate of the earlier work.

With *Das Marienleben* (The Life of Mary), op. 27 (1923), an hourlong song-cycle to fifteen poems by Rainer Maria Rilke, it was suddenly clear that Hindemith's period of experiment was over. He had absorbed or discarded what his seniors had to offer him and now spoke a new musical language with undoubted authority. This work heralds the first, the neo-classical period of his maturity.

Although an unexpected tenderness is revealed on occasion, the predominant impression is of a language deliberately unromantic in character, with little by way of 'illustration' and even less of colour. The voice's capacity for lingering emotional emphasis is seldom exploited and the vocal line becomes an extension of the spare clear lines of the piano. The piano part is crucial, for it is here that his now contrapuntal imagination can work freely. Counterpoint also provides the environment in which the lowest part is released from the role of harmonic bass, and can take its place in a texture whose relationship with functional harmony is remote. The following example, from the ninth song, 'Von der Hochzeit zu Kana' (The Wedding at Cana), will illustrate how a section can be defined by a firm tonal basis while depending for its momentum on the vigour of the rhythmic interplay, the strength of the individual lines, and the metallic harmonic clashes. Hindemith's predilection for diatonic intervals contributes to the relative familiarity of the sound and also to the lack of harmonic function, since there are few leading-note progressions.

Ex.5

(Mässig schnelle Halbe)

The omnipresence of counterpoint gives rise to rhythmic patterns and formal structures based on eighteenth-century models, rather than on the declamatory rhythms and free forms associated with expressionism. The passacaglia of the second song, the ritornello-concerto of the fifth, the variations of the fourteenth, provide instances of the formal types that now find a place in his music.

The richly varied idiom of *Das Marienleben* is not entirely consistent, as is only to be expected in a work of such length and diversity. When Hindemith ties himself to a mainly harmonic means of expression a certain crudity results. This is most obvious in 'Geburt Christi' (The Birth of Christ), a song which was rewritten for the 1948 revision of the cycle.

Ex.6

But when the melodic line has greater intrinsic interest, the crudity is less obtrusive. In the revision he retained the original melodic ideas for thirteen of the fifteen songs.

NEO-CLASSICISM AND *GEBRAUCHSMUSIK*

HINDEMITH'S reputation as an *enfant terrible* now faded away and his prominent position in musical life was placed on a more respectable basis. It was consolidated by his extraordinary versatility. While the flow of compositions continued unabated, he was increasingly occupied as a performer (either with the Amar Quartet or as a solo viola or viola d'amore player), and having joined the Donaueschingen Festival committee in 1923 he also became something of an entrepreneur. For Donaueschingen he commissioned new scores for specific media rather than fill out the programmes with the substandard ones already submitted. In this way he preserved the festival's prestige. In 1927 he added teaching to this network of activities, accepting an invitation from Franz Schreker to take up an appointment as Professor of Composition at the Hochschule für Musik in Berlin. He had no teaching experience, but once his initial hesitations were overcome he immediately grappled with two major, interlinked problems: how to answer student requests to 'explain' contemporary music and his own in particular, and how to provide contemporary music suitable for amateurs. The first was to lead to the eventual publication of the theoretical work *The Craft of Musical Composition*, and the second to the *Sing- und Spielmusik* (Music to Sing and Play), usually known as *Gebrauchsmusik*. Both contributed profoundly towards the growth of the idiom which was to succeed his neo-classicism and become characteristic of him for the rest of his life.

*　　　　*　　　　*

Neo-classicism was a reaction against what then seemed to be the hypersensitivity and egocentricity of late romanticism, against a language which in the social conditions following the 1914–18 war appeared irrelevant. Most composers at that time were responsive to the new call for objectivity. As a native of the country which had given birth to romanticism and which now suffered most acutely from the effects of war, Hindemith's own response was especially intense. Since he had, as it were, been born to neo-classicism, it is not surprising that features of his neo-classical music should become deeply rooted in his creative personality. A distaste for self-indulgent expression and an emphasis on clarity of line, texture, and form remained typical of him throughout his life. Another feature is an affinity with baroque music, and particularly the music of Bach—that is, with a language not directed primarily towards the expression of 'personal feelings'. To draw inspiration from music of other historical periods (though not exclusively the baroque) also remained typical of him.

The majority of Hindemith's neo-classical music is for small instrumental groups. As an instrumentalist himself, he was anxious to rescue his colleagues from the obscurity of the orchestra pit,[1] and the medium is far removed from the literary association and subjectivity inherent in vocal music. His approach is conveniently illustrated in the seven concerti grossi collectively titled *Kammermusik*. These comprise the

[1] There were further reasons. The Amar Quartet was by now much in demand and Hindemith was therefore encouraged to supplement their repertoire—hence the composition of the masterly Quartet no. 4, op. 32 (1923), and the String Trio no. 1, op. 34 (1924).

concerto for chamber orchestra (not so called by Hindemith, but such by implication) already mentioned and six solo concertos, for piano, cello, violin, viola, viola d'amore, and organ. As evidence of his concern for the player, most parts in a *Kammermusik* are solo parts. The actual soloist is *primus inter pares*. Hindemith's scoring accentuates the individual lines rather than creating classically blended sonorities, and for this reason gives prominence to the sharp timbres of wind and brass instruments. His inside knowledge of instruments is especially apparent in his writing for strings (which accounts, for example, for the private joke between composer and performer in the march movement of the *Kammermusik nr. 4*—a quotation from Paganini's B flat Caprice), even though their natural tendency towards an expressive cantabile is kept in check. Yet his instrumental facility had its drawbacks. While reluctant to reach beyond the conventional sound resources (the use of fluttertonguing, col legno, etc., was essentially foreign to him) he nevertheless set up on occasion what appear to be deliberately *outré* combinations of instruments which would of their own accord stimulate new ideas and avoid the routine figurations likely to be prompted by the instincts of the practising musician. At all events this interpretation accounts for some extremely individual scoring in, for example, the *Kammermusik nr. 4* calling for two piccolos, two clarinets (E flat and B flat) and a bass clarinet, two bassoons and a double bassoon, cornet, trombone, and tuba, four each of violas, cellos, and basses, and four small drums—an ensemble which makes itself felt with startling effect in the opening movement, headed 'Signal'. Here, piercing wind trills and cornet fanfares over a lurching bass splendidly arouse expectation for the entry of the solo violin.

The concertante element resulting from this instrumental approach, allied to imitative textures, ostinato rhythms, and rigidly defined phrase structure, is responsible for the hectic, unrelenting activity of so many neo-classical works. This is indeed their most striking characteristic, and the one which distinguishes them most readily from the more relaxed expression of contemporary neo-classical music, and from their baroque models. The Bach of the Brandenburg Concerto no. 6 may hover over this excerpt from the *Kammermusik nr. 5*, but the sheer energy of Hindemith's music is so arresting that Bach remains only a nebulous presence (Ex. 7).

The uniformity of mood in the individual movement, to all intents and purposes repudiating the give and take of human speech, is offset by carefully controlled contrasts between movements. Almost all *Kammermusik* works start with a flourish, an introductory call to attention. What follows depends on the length of this first movement. In the *Kammermusik nr.* 2 Hindemith was not absolutely confident of his method, for the slow movement which follows the opening two-part invention does not by its nature supply the release of energy demanded,

Ex.7

the answer to the question posed. The more balanced proportions of subsequent works give them a certain lightness of touch, especially in their endings. The whirlwind pianissimo finale of the *Kammermusik nr.* 4, for example, is a unique phenomenon, an admirable foil to the preceding march and trio, and quite unlike anything else in musical literature (unless one cites the finale of Hindemith's own unaccompanied Violin Sonata, op. 31, no. 1).

The quintessence of these works is to be found in the Concerto for Orchestra, op. 38 (1925), Hindemith's first work for full orchestra. To preserve the necessary distinction of timbre he grouped the orchestra into families, or split it up sometimes into small concertini—a method anticipating that of many later composers. In the short first movement, the ritornello theme is first announced by the strings, then by the brass, then by the strings again. The episodes are given to a concertino consisting of oboe, bassoon, and violin. The same principle applies in the second movement, and in the last, a passacaglia consisting of forty-seven repetitions of a six-note theme upon which carefully ordered divisions build up in two waves to a jubilant final chord of E flat. In this *tour de force* Hindemith extends the possibilities of his method by using a great variety of performing techniques within the families. The remaining movement in the Concerto, the third, is scored for wind alone, and is a fine instance of another Hindemithian speciality associated with the revival of baroque forms—movements in march tempo. Accompanimental trills on wind instruments in high register, a characteristic feature of his scoring, obviously derive from his liking for marches and military music.

The monothematic forms used in the Concerto are typical of his neo-classical period, as is the work's relationship to tonality. Hindemith's music can never be considered atonal, but it came close to it at this time. Precisely how close may be gauged from the following example from the Concerto, the opening sentence of the first movement (whose courante rhythm, incidentally, incorporates the traditional hemiola at the end of the second sentence).

Ex.8

The music begins and ends in an unequivocal D major: tonality, or at any rate the triad, remains an indispensable structural support and vividly so, when thus allied to essentially non-triadic 'harmony'. There are, moreover, clear tonal elements within the individual lines. But the rhythmic accents of the main lines (the two outer ones) rarely coincide and the listener is forced to separate them. When they do, the *intervals* of sevenths and ninths (as at the places marked with an asterisk) are heard and not the harmony which might be associated with them. Towards the end of the sentence there is a significant increase in tonal clarity. Hindemith's 'harmony' thus can be summarized as a deliberate use of dissonant intervals to establish tensions which in the context of powerful diatonic elements demand resolution and which, in the structural upbeats, get it. Hindemith himself came to regard this lack of functional progression as a weakness, but we may well admire the rough-hewn vitality of such music.

In *Cardillac*, op. 39 (1926), Hindemith's first full-length opera and undoubtedly his major achievement of the period, the neo-classical style is put to remarkable dramatic effect. It may seem surprising that he should have turned to opera when his language was not conventionally 'dramatic' and that he should then have chosen a subject which, in its exploration of the darker regions of human behaviour, is expressionistic. But opera was in his bones. In *Cardillac* he transferred his apparently unyielding style from the concert hall to the theatre with extraordinary panache. Its urgency of expression has, in fact, benefited from the transfer. 'Active' music prospers in active surroundings: and Ferdinand Lion, his librettist, certainly placed the emphasis on action rather than reflection. The attraction of the E. T. A. Hoffmann short story *Das Fräulein von Scuderi* was strong enough to overcome any hesitations about an expressionistic subject. It dealt with a theme which was to hold a life-long fascination for him: the nature of the artist.

Cardillac, the goldsmith, represents the artist/craftsman in an extreme form—as a man so preoccupied with his jewellery and so indifferent to human relationships and social values that he will even murder for the sake of his work. He kills his customers in order to recover their purchases. Hindemith himself stands aside from the behaviour of his central figure, who, except in the ambiguous final scene, is neither condoned nor condemned. This objectivity is maintained in the presentation of the characters (none of whom, except Cardillac, have personal names), in the lack of character development, the subordination of the love interest and, particularly, in the musical construction. Lion recast the original story drastically[2] and provided a succession of situations each concentrating on a precise mood which could be supported by the purely musical logic of the forms used in Hindemith's instrumental music and also of those deriving from baroque opera—da capo aria, scena, recitative. Although other composers, notably Berg in *Wozzeck*, had used classical forms in opera at this time, Hindemith was by far the most uncompromising in method, because his are so clearly audible. These forms do not, as is sometimes

---

[2] The Fräulein of the title does not appear at all. Her function as the one person to whom Cardillac can entrust his work is revived in the 1952 revision of the opera.

suggested, ride roughshod over the stage action. The passacaglias, for example, at the end of Act 2, when Cardillac resolves to recover the chain bought by the Officer, and near the end of the opera when the crowd extort a confession of guilt, are apt symbols of the inevitability of these situations. And no one could mistake the da capo aria for the Daughter in Act 2, with its concertante parts for oboe, violin, and horn, nor fail to respond to its evocation of her unease.

Ex.9

Such application of self-contained musical forms to highly dramatic purpose makes *Cardillac* one of the landmarks of twentieth-century opera.

Its success on the stage is due to the flair with which Hindemith seized the opportunities for theatrical effect. The 'pantomime' at the end of Act 1—a delicate invention for two flutes and muted pizzicato strings accompanying the silent scene between the Lady and the Cavalier—provides the most celebrated example of Hindemith's *savoir faire*. To dash expectations of a love duet and then produce something better requires more than average expertise. There is also the nicely judged dramatic irony of the background music, a beery café ragtime, while the Officer anxiously awaits Cardillac at the beginning of Act 3.

As if to demonstrate his professional adaptability, the two other operas of the period are on comic themes, and both briefly recall the irreverent young Hindemith. *Hin und Zurück* (There and Back) was written for the 1927 Baden-Baden Festival (the successor to Donaueschingen) which featured one-act chamber operas. It is a sparkling little piece which proceeds to the point at which the jealous husband shoots his wife and then, by the intervention of a benevolent *deus ex machina*, reverses the action, ending as it had begun with the deaf aunt sitting quietly knitting. Hindemith's music does not mirror the action to the extent of working in retrograde after mid-point; it reverses the sequence of its sections, an operation entailing some delicate grafting. The libretto was written by Marcellus Schiffer, a leading figure of Berlin cabaret of the 1920s—a fact which will explain the opera's subtitle of 'Sketch'.

Schiffer also wrote the libretto for *Neues vom Tage* (News of the Day), a full-length satire. It hits out, in thorough German fashion, at a multitude of targets—journalism, show business, commerce, the art craze, opera, divorce. The hero and heroine, Edward and Laura, want to get divorced. They have to employ a professional 'grounds for divorce', the beautiful Mr. Hermann, who tends to exceed his brief. Edward, incensed, smashes a priceless Venus at a museum where a tryst had been arranged and Laura is disturbed in her bath by Hermann. These activities put Edward in jail and debt, but also in the headlines. He accepts an offer to appear with Laura in cabaret in a short number recounting their late behaviour. This is a great success, they become solvent again and privately decide not to get divorced after all. Their public image, however, now fixed for good, will permit no such thing.

Neues vom Tage is not completely successful, even on its own rather limited satiric-cum-documentary terms. The complexity of the music tends to smother the essentially simple plot. But as a period piece it is quite as entertaining as *Hin und Zurück*. Schiffer's hand is clearly seen in the sketchlike nature of several of the short scenes: the climactic scene is, in fact, a real cabaret number. Standard operatic items are caricatured. Thus, instead of a Love Duet there is what amounts to a Hate Duet (in foxtrot tempo with the refrain 'we are going to get divorced'); for good measure, a Kitsch Duet is fitted in later. Instead of the arioso in praise of the beloved, there is an arioso in praise of constant hot water (this the beginning of the bath scene), accompanied by two solo violins and four string quartets (violin, viola, cello, and bass), two of them muted. There is a chorus of Typewriter Girls (a most skilful conception this, with xylophone, solo piano, and piano duet contributing to the clicking texture). The frequent jazz inflections are affectionately appropriate to the subject-matter. The Act 1 Quartet, for example, offers a charming example of a blues waltz. The cabaret number, on the other hand, has an added purpose: it is a rather heavy-handed parody of Weill, complete with alto saxophone, mandoline, banjo, and piano.

The other 'opera' of this period was *Lehrstück* (Lesson), for which Hindemith's original intention was that his librettist Brecht should write something involving the audience (and particularly the music critics). Brecht accommodated this startling idea. He even expanded it, by conceiving the work as a succession of apparently unrelated elements also including mime (or film), narration, and a clown scene punctuated by an off-stage brass band. The main purpose of a Brechtian Lehrstück, however, was not so much to create a pioneer work of musical theatre (as this one has, in fact, proved to be) as to put across a proposition. In this case there are several—idealism is of no use unless it is for the common good; if the individual dies in pursuit of such idealism, that also is of no account; salvation is to be understood in terms of submission and 'consent'. The provocative staging and Brecht's aggressively political outlook deeply annoyed Hindemith, who refused to collaborate on a revised version of the work.[3] For him the work was neither an experiment nor an occasion for polemics. He merely set the text to music which, as his remarks in the preface to the published piano score make clear, was less important than the opportunities it provided for large-scale communal music-making.

This was indeed the main point of *Lehrstück*, his most substantial piece in the genre known as *Gebrauchsmusik*, perhaps best translated as 'Useful Music'. (In the preface to *A Composer's World*, Cambridge, Mass., 1952, Hindemith assures his readers that the English equivalents are no more hideous than the German original.) Hindemith was by temperament an ensemble player, and it was natural that a large proportion of his output should be written as much for the performer as for

---

[3] Brecht made a cutting reference to Hindemith in the Appendix to the published revised version, *Das Badener Lehrstück vom Einverständnis*. The original text is available only in the piano score of *Lehrstück*.

the audience. But by the mid-twenties he realized that neither this nor the aesthetic considerations behind his neo-classical music were in themselves likely to check the growing isolation of the contemporary composer. More deliberate measures were needed, which took account of the root causes of this isolation. In 1927 he wrote: 'A composer should write today only if he knows for what purpose he is writing. The days of composing for the sake of composing are perhaps gone forever. On the other hand the demand for music is so great that the composer and the consumer ought most emphatically to come at least to an understanding.' This text was often cited as a *Gebrauchsmusik* manifesto and as such occasioned much ridicule. The familiar misinterpretation was, as Hindemith wrote himself, that *Gebrauchsmusik* relied on the 'tritest relationship between cause and effect in music'. Less epigramatically, he surely meant that the obscurities and difficulties of contemporary music arose from an 'art for art's sake' philosophy, and that they would be reduced if composers directed their talents towards less personal and more realistic ends. Thus he wrote music for mechanical instruments, films, and radio. More particularly, he wrote to provide opportunities for experiences (of playable, accessible music) upon which an understanding of contemporary music could be based. In other words, he took the view that musical health depended substantially on nourishing amateur players. *Gebrauchsmusik* was primarily amateur music, and a heroic attempt to revive the relationship between composer, performer, and listener which had flourished before the nineteenth century. The Nazis put an end to his active work in this field, but much of the music he wrote after 1933 demonstrated that *Gebrauchsmusik* was not a pragmatic episode but an integral part of his interpretation of the composer's function.

Hindemith had given some idea of how his attitudes were to develop when, for the Donaueschingen festivals of 1925 and 1926, he commissioned music for, respectively, unaccompanied chorus and military band (an ensemble hitherto unknown to 'serious' music)—two choices which obviously reflected the practising musician's anxiety that the festival was becoming limited to a clique. By contributing to these two festivals himself, with the *Lieder nach alten Texten*, op. 33, and the *Konzertmusik* for wind band, op. 41, he attempted a cure. The style of both works remained typical of his neo-classical music; but their *raison d'être* was a pointer in the direction of *Gebrauchsmusik*. (In 1936 he revised the op. 33 choruses. In their new form, *Five Songs on Old Texts*, they are one of the most enjoyable and approachable twentieth-century works of their kind.)

His first music for mechanical instruments was written in 1926. At that time Hindemith saw in it a means by which the 'emotional' gestures he disliked could be eliminated. This included a Toccata for player piano (a work impossible to play on a conventional piano) and the score for the 1926 version of Schlemmer's *Triadic Ballet*[4] written for a small mechanical organ. Mechanical music for use with films included music for the cartoon *Felix the Cat at the Circus*, shown in the section of the 1927 Baden-Baden festival set aside for film music, and for Hans Richter's surrealistic film *Vormittagsspuk* (Ghosts at Breakfast). It may be noted that the idea for *Hin und Zurück* was obviously suggested by contemporary film techniques. He also regarded the writing of film music as a valuable compositional discipline and at the Hochschule set up a Studio for Mechanical Music. Mechanical music was to be a short-lived phenomenon because the instruments themselves lost their commercial value with the advent of the gramophone and the sound-track. He published none of it, but his interest in new instruments and media persisted. In 1928 he gave a new lease of life to the heckelphone by writing a Trio, with piano and viola. In 1929 he wrote, in collaboration with Weill, *Der Lindberghflug*,[5] a radio cantata with a specially written text by Brecht, based on Lindbergh's solo flight across the Atlantic. In 1931 he wrote a *Konzertmusik* for trautonium and strings. (The trautonium was an electronic instrument designed by Friedrich Trautwein, one of Hindemith's colleagues at the Hochschule, who directed a class in acoustics.)

His first music for amateurs was written in 1927. This was the *Spielmusik* for strings, flutes, and oboes, op. 43, no. 1. The composition of this work was stimulated by a visit to a 'working week' of the musical *Jugendbewegung* (already a flourishing movement owing most of its drive to Fritz Jöde, who was later to collaborate with Hindemith in the publication of amateur music). It and its companion in op. 43, tiny three-part choruses, initiated a close connection between the movement and contemporary music. There were reciprocal advantages. Hindemith himself renewed contact with early polyphonic music and German folk-song (the staple diet of the *Jugendbewegung*). The *Spielmusik* was followed by several other works including *Lehrstück*, the children's opera, *Wir bauen eine Stadt* (Let's build a Town) and the *Plöner Musiktag* (Day of Music at Plön) (1932), material for a complete day's

---

[4] Oscar Schlemmer was one of the major figures of the Bauhaus. His ballet, conceived as a sequence of moods progressing from the playful to the serious, was first performed in 1922.
[5] The published *Der Lindberghflug* is the second version, for which Weill alone wrote the music.

music-making. Not all of them avoid a certain alfresco heartiness, but their notably un-eclectic language and their general expertise is self-evident. The following extract from *Wir bauen eine Stadt*, perfectly tailored to the accomplishments and inclinations of primary school children, shows the extent to which Hindemith adapted his style to the demands of amateur music. As in much of the other *Gebrauchsmusik*, the instrumentation accommodates what players are available.

Ex.10

* Add town as appropriate

Such simplification does not only affirm his practicality; nor does it merely throw out the asperities, leaving nothing much behind. Rather is it a stage in the fashioning of a new idiom.

The first major evidence of this came with the three magnificent *Konzertmusik* works of 1930, for viola and orchestra, for piano, brass, and two harps, and for brass and strings. They are distinguished from their predecessors, the *Kammermusik* series, by a lyric melody whose vocal contours and strongly tonal bias stem ultimately from German folk-music. This is most clearly illustrated in the central episode of the rondo finale of the second of them, where a genuine folk-song, 'Reiters Abschied' (used again in the last movement of the Organ Sonata no. 3), glides in quite unobtrusively. Hindemith's music now breathes; the ear can grasp the separate components of long phrases and sentences. It also becomes harmonic, in the traditional sense that harmonies provide support for both the melodic line and the total structure. A consequence of this emphasis on melody and harmony is that contrapuntal textures become less pervasive and at the same time more purposeful, since they can be introduced with a greater degree of contrast. Fugatos, for example, appear more frequently.

Each of the *Konzertmusik* works has a distinct character. The first is a divertimento-like Viola Concerto. Hindemith here marvellously communicates his sheer delight in composing music. The second, although of exactly the same length, sounds a larger work because its moods are more diverse. Hindemith does not combine the brass and harps, except in the slow introduction and at the end of the work where the effect of the crystalline textures of the setting of 'Reiters Abschied' (Ex. 11) is to

calm the roisterous high spirits and lead them into a hushed communion.
The work is constructed in two parts, the first an introduction and

Ex.11 (Mässig schnell)

allegro, the second a set of variations followed by a rondo. This formal
plan is adopted in the *Konzertmusik* for brass and strings. Here the first
part is an allegro with lento coda (a powerful extension of the main
allegro theme), the second a fugal allegro with slow central section.

*   *   *

It was perhaps inevitable that Hindemith should sooner or later turn
to the old form of oratorio. He could hardly have failed to be drawn to
the erudite and strangely lyrical verse of Gottfried Benn, especially as a
chance hearing of a radio discussion between Benn and Brecht about
whether the artist can influence society revealed Benn as the antithesis
of Brecht. But it is difficult to believe that he could have identified
himself wholly with the nihilistic vision of *Das Unaufhörliche* (1931),
even if its central idea was to become a crucial aspect of *Mathis der
Maler*. Benn's standpoint commended itself no doubt as much for its
repudiation of the Brechtian credo as for its own sake. As if to underline
this, Hindemith quotes almost literally the music accompanying the
clown scene in *Lehrstück* in the ironical baritone solo in Part 2 of the
oratorio 'Aber die Fortschritte der modernen Technik!' (The progress
of modern science!). The collaboration with Benn is therefore of considerable significance: Hindemith is now more prudent in his choice of
texts and text-writers.

Benn wrote an introduction to his oratorio text in which he described
'Das Unaufhörliche' as the elemental, unceasing (unaufhörlich) law of
creation—namely, that everything is in a constant state of transforma-
tion. Part 1 of the oratorio draws a picture of the inexorable strength of
this principle. Part 2 catalogues rebellious human reactions to it. Love,
knowledge, science, art, religion—are not these perpetually valid? The

reply is that they are all transitory: nothing can redeem Man from dark fatal thoughts of Das Unaufhörliche. Part 3 considers how Man should live with it. Benn's answer is given by the Boy's Chorus: suffering will conquer it. The man who submits will himself become part of Das Unaufhörliche.

The massive proportions of the text demanded musical ideas of comparable breadth and Hindemith's new style supplied appropriate material. But faced with the problems of writing for a large amateur chorus he fell back on conventional four-part textures and the first manifestation of that noble but rather characterless idiom which was to mar some of his later music. Possibly the absence of drama, and certainly the daunting prospect of giving musical substance to huge areas of text accounts for the lack of significant detail in this score. The following typical example sounds more like a flowing counterpoint to a principle melody not stated, than a melody in its own right.

Ex.12

No.5 (Ruhig gehend, sehr gehalten)

His next important work, the Philharmonic Concerto (written for the fiftieth anniversary of the Berlin Philharmonic Orchestra), although couched in the same idiom, is greatly superior because Hindemith's imagination has been stimulated by a more congenial purpose—of giving momentary prominence to each member of the orchestra. The penultimate variation for string trio with full orchestra (the work is a theme and variations) is one of his most breathtaking inspirations.

MATHIS DER MALER AND THE LATER MUSIC

By nominating Hindemith for the advisory committee of the Reichsmusikkammer (the music division of the Nazi chamber of culture), as representative of the younger generation, the Nazis hoped he might become an acceptable and conformist musical leader. They took some time to realize that he was unlikely to become 'gleichgeschaltet' (conformist). Hindemith himself could scarcely believe that Germany would remain hypnotized for much longer. The announcement in November 1934 by the Kulturgemeinde, an organization dedicated to the spiritual education of the Nazi party, of a boycott on performances of his music came therefore, in spite of previous agitation in the Nazi press, as something of a surprise and roused Wilhelm Furtwängler into a passionate yet reasoned defence of Hindemith. Furtwängler had conducted in March 1934 the outstandingly successful first performance of the Symphony *Mathis der Maler*. The Hindemith Case now became a public issue. Furtwängler resigned from his conducting and administrative posts.[1] Hindemith found himself denounced in the customary jargon and was the object of a scathing personal attack by Goebbels, who took as his text the bath scene from *Neues vom Tage*. Still unable to accept that the Nazis could remain in power and concerned that leaving his country would sap his creative energy, Hindemith did not give up his Berlin home at once. The Nazis treated him with circumspection. Apart from an enforced 'leave of absence' in early 1935, he was not actually prevented from teaching at the Hochschule. His music was still printed. He was allowed to make concert tours abroad and to fulfil a contract with the Turkish Government.[2] The Kulturgemeinde boycott was not endorsed by the Reichsmusikkammer (there was some rivalry between the two organizations) until

[1] Furtwängler made his peace with the Nazis a year later. Hindemith never forgot Furtwängler's support and wrote a moving obituary tribute to him in 1954 (*Gedenkworte für Wilhelm Furtwängler*, Heidelberg, 1955).

[2] This rather quixotic undertaking was to build up a thriving and organized musical life in Turkey. Hindemith set about the task with a real administrative flair, drawing up a comprehensive plan and engaging European musicians, both performers and theorists (and instrument makers) in sufficient numbers to establish standards, but not such as to smother native talent. He spent periods in Turkey between 1934 and 1937.

the autumn of 1937 and thus the occasional Hindemith performance did take place. But eventually, in 1938, he left Germany for Switzerland and, after finding it impossible to make a living there, emigrated to the United States in 1940. Emigration had little effect on his style. In the United States he found himself in a position which in the circumstances could hardly have been bettered. He returned to teaching, in the rarefied 'European' atmosphere of Yale University, where he became Professor of Music Theory, and lived in the cosmopolitan town of New Haven. As if to express his gratitude to the country which sheltered him, he devoted extraordinary care to teaching[3] and furthermore kindled an enthusiasm for the performance of old music on authentic instruments which revealed him to be almost as valuable an acquisition for this alone. After the 1939–45 war he refused many offers to return to Germany and indeed strengthened ties with the United States. He became an American citizen in 1946 and in 1949–50 gave a series of lectures at Harvard Univesity which formed the basis of *A Composer's World*, perhaps the most profound and thorough analysis of the composer's position ever written. In *Johann Sebastian Bach*[4] he did something to allay the disappointment of those who felt that the earlier book had revealed too little of his own character. By interpreting the prevailing 'melancholy' of the music Bach wrote in the last ten years of his life as the price the composer must pay for having reached the ultimate in technical perfection, he clearly drew parallels with his own position. The melancholy of his own late music is, however, the result not so much of the impossibility of proceeding further (as with Bach) as of the sense if not of rejection at least of isolation. After the war it was clear that his erstwhile position as guide and mentor to the younger generation of composers was no longer secure. In 1951 he accepted the position of Professor of Music at Zürich University while remaining on the staff at Yale, and for two academic years divided his time between the universities, eventually resigning from Yale in 1953. In that year he settled in the village of Blonay, overlooking Lake Geneva. He gave up regular teaching in 1957 in order to concentrate on composition and to foster his new-found enthusiasm for conducting. He died on 28 December 1963, in Frankfurt, where he had begun his career.

*   *   *

[3] Some idea of his meticulous methods may be deduced from the textbooks he produced in America—*Elementary Training for Musicians* (London, rev. ed. 1949) and the two books entitled *Traditional Harmony*.

[4] *Johann Sebastian Bach: Tradition and Heritage* (London, 1952).

There is some irony in the fact that the Nazi campaign was associated with the Symphony *Mathis der Maler*, for the palpably German qualities of the work are unmistakable. But while the music of the Symphony could conceivably have been upheld as a model for the German composer of the Hitler period, the text of the opera could not. Numerous overt references point to an indictment of Nazi doctrine, notably the burning of Lutheran literature in Scene 4, which recalls the Nazi burning of 'politically and morally un-German writings' on 10 May 1933. Furtwängler was not permitted to stage the work.

To dwell on the political factors behind the opera's creation would, however, be to misinterpret. If Hindemith's thesis had been political he would have been more straightforward about it. In fact, one of the lessons of *Mathis* is that the artist is *not* competent to dabble in politics. The opera goes far deeper and is more universalized. It is an allegory about the artist, his doubts, his aspirations. For whom are works of art created? What is their purpose? This central theme is given authority by the historical facts of Matthias Grünewald and his famous Isenheim Altarpiece, of Albrecht, Archbishop of Mainz, the Peasant's Revolt and the birth-throes of the Reformation; furthermore Hindemith's roots were in the countryside around Mainz, where the opera is set. By writing his own text he emphasized its autobiographical aspects. It is indeed a personal testament.

Mathis, brooding over the apparent triviality of his art, opts for a life of action, siding with the peasants in their war against the princes and the Church and, consequently, against his patron, Albrecht. But he finds himself powerless to help his fellow men, and the peasants, revealed as cruel and unscrupulous, are defeated. In his disillusionment he is possessed by visions. He imagines himself as St. Anthony and the main figures in his life appear in symbolic form to tempt and torment him. But they are insignificant compared with the animal representations of his inner conflicts (as in the Isenheim panel 'The Temptation of St. Anthony'), which now drive him to despair. Albrecht in the guise of St. Paul (as in another panel 'St. Paul and St. Anthony in the Wilderness') tells him that he can best serve God and his fellow men by nourishing the talents he has been given, with reverence and humility. He should not question their value—'the tree knows not of its fruit'. Albrecht's final command is to 'go out and create'. (Hindemith's word here is carefully chosen: the German 'bilden' has many connotations—to create, paint, teach, to be an example.) His suppressed energies now release a flood of masterpieces. In the last scene of the opera Mathis, having drained himself of all he can give, packs his few belongings in a chest and resigns himself to death. *Mathis der Maler* testifies to the profound change in idiom and outlook that had first broken surface with the *Konzertmusik* works of 1930. The composer who had hitherto espoused almost any workable musical enterprise with equal and apparently indiscriminate relish now fades into history. In *Mathis* it is as if Hindemith had been confronted with himself and at the moment of recognition suddenly realized what his real nature was. Although the opera contains scenes of violent action with music of corresponding tension, the final impression is of a serenity and ease of expression very rare in twentieth-century music, and of which only fleeting glimpses had been offered in his previous works. This quality is as easy to sense as it is difficult to account for. An explanation may lie in the fact that the Nazis forced a degree of introspection on the naturally active Hindemith. It may also be connected with the closeness of his links with German folk-music. One may see more than coincidence in this identification with the roots of his musical inheritance at a time when political tyranny was distorting it beyond recognition.

The most prominent folk-music quotation is of 'Es sungen drei Engel ein süsser Gesang' (Three angels sang a sweet song). Although it appears in only two sections of the opera and is in itself very short, this beautiful melody exerts an uncanny spell over the whole work. Its first appearance is in the prelude, headed 'Engelkonzert' (Concert of Angels)—an evocation of the preternatural ecstasy of that panel from the Isenheim Altarpiece depicting three angels playing to the Virgin. The folk-song dominates the introductory section and reappears at the climax of the following allegro (which has three main themes, one for each angel). It returns in the first part of Scene 6 in which Mathis consoles the frightened Regina, whose father, Schwalb, leader of the peasants, has been killed in the war. Mathis describes his vision of the 'Engelkonzert', the music recalling with even greater luminosity the elation of the prelude. The other prominent folk-music quotation is of the familiar 'Lobt Gott Ihr Christen allzugleich', the Lutheran rallying-cry, which is used very dramatically during Mathis's duet with Ursula in Scene 4.

Whatever the sources of this new freedom of utterance in *Mathis*, there is no doubt that it lends itself to a wide variety of expression. This is most clearly seen in the characterization of the four principal roles, Mathis, Albrecht, Ursula, and Regina. Regina's music is the simplest. Hindemith skilfully traces her development from innocent child in Scene 1 (where the naïveté of the folk-song 'Es vollt ein Maidlein waschen gehn' is peculiarly apt) to the infinitely pathetic creature of Scene 6 who has come to know the horrors of life before her time.

Ex.13

The impulsive Ursula is more complex. With unusual psychological insight Hindemith has created a character embodying both the passionate possessive lover, as in Scene 3:

Ex.14

and the self-sacrificing idealist, as in Scene 5. Here she is prepared to offer herself as bride to Albrecht, whose marriage could then be a powerful instrument in the hands of the Lutherans. Albrecht's refusal stings her to accuse him hotly of irresponsibility in condoning Lutheranism, and thus she is the agent through whom the liberal, hedonistic archbishop learns that he must stand by his church. His self-respect regained, he is able in the final part of Scene 6 to help Mathis to *his* self-respect.

The development of Mathis's personality is traced with equal subtlety. In Scene 1 his doubts are reflected in the unsettled musical expression, ranging from the wayward phrases of the opening section ('Is what you create enough?') to the fatherly response to Regina and the deferential aping of Schwalb at the close. In the subsequent scenes he shows reserves of will-power strong enough to overcome his love for Ursula and conversely such as to bring him to desperation, when his encounter with the peasants has proved futile.

This side of his character is revealed more fully in the second part of Scene 6, and especially in that section where Ursula in the guise of beggar, whore, and martyr appears to torment him. Hindemith did not rise to the challenge of a scene depicting Mathis at work. But the proud resignation of the final scene leaves no doubt of the intervening spate of creative activity. This scene is in two parts. After the first, in which Regina dies, there is an interlude headed 'Grablegung' (as in another Isenheim panel, of Christ's entombment). This ostensibly is a requiem for Regina, but the same music returns with added poignancy in the closing pages of the opera as a background to the halting but deliberate phrases of Mathis as he packs his belongings away.

Hindemith's treatment of character in *Mathis* may be said to be conventional, as may his use of aria, ensemble, and chorus within a gradual tightening or relaxation of dramatic tension—this a noticeable change from the defiantly self-contained forms of *Cardillac*. Clear musical forms do, however, underlie *Mathis*. Their unostentatious use and particularly the masterly transitions conceal their presence in such a way as to focus attention on the human rather than the musical sphere, which is one of the reasons why *Mathis* is the better opera. Whether its near-Wagnerian relationship between music and drama makes it less 'theatrical' is a moot point. It has few of the obvious operatic appurtenances—abrupt changes of mood, dominance of love interest, heroic action, and so on—and its novelties (the scene of the visions and the daring valedictory final scene) slip into the dramatic framework without fuss. Yet Hindemith's dramatic integrity has created as moving a theatrical experience as any offered in twentieth-century opera.

As with the opera, the Symphony *Mathis der Maler* marks a turning-point in his career. Here it is possible to be more specific about the change. Simply by heading the work 'Symphony' Hindemith announces that after nearly a decade of music attuned to the baroque era, he now comes to terms with his classical and romantic heritage. Moreover, by heading the three movements 'Engelkonzert', 'Grablegung' and 'Die Versuchung des heiligen Antonius' (The Temptation of St. Anthony[5] —the only movement not lifted bodily from the opera) and not attempting to disguise the programmatic inspiration and apparently piecemeal construction, the erstwhile anti-romantic lays claim to follow one of the foremost banners of romanticism. The work's triumphant affirmation of classical and romantic tradition is evident in several details; in the wealth of thematic material, the metamorphosis from conflict to grandeur in the finale, elaborate thematic transformations in the same movement, and orchestral textures which with tonal and often triadic harmony acquire a homogeneity quite foreign to the block sonorities of, for example, the Philharmonic Concerto. But the most decisive link with these traditions is effected by the new harmonic language. Although Hindemith had been developing in this direction since 1930, the impli-

[5] For this last movement, which amounts to a précis of the second and third parts of Scene 6, Hindemith provides the motto 'Ubi eras, Jhesu bone, ubi eras? Quare non affuisti ut saneres vulnera mea?' (Where were you, good Jesus? Why did you not come and heal my wounds?) These words, uttered by Mathis at the darkest moment in the scene, are inscribed on the painting. Their setting in the opera is not included in the symphony. The phrases which punctuate them are, however. These are from the Latin sequence *Lauda Sion Salvatorem*, whose association with the festival of Corpus Christi adds a further dimension to Hindemith's symbolism.

cations of this language were not fully realized until the *Mathis* Symphony. Here tonality again acts as a crucial structural support and sonata form again becomes a valid formal archetype. It is no coincidence that the Symphony marks the renaissance of the Austro-German symphonic tradition, at a time when that tradition was widely believed to have been made obsolete by the harmonic innovations of the early twentieth century. (It is also one of the first of an important body of twentieth-century concert works derived from operas.)

The tenets of Hindemith's harmonic language were expounded in *The Craft of Musical Composition* (1934–6).[6] In order to understand the most important of them, how they operate in the *Mathis* Symphony and how they control the interdependence of its movements, it is necessary first to give a brief summary of the book. It is substantially the product of his needs as a teacher (although it may also be seen as the product of a deeper need for order and rationality). His main object is to seek out an organized musical language which will embrace both twentieth-century harmonic developments and the vocabulary of traditional harmony. He approaches the problem via acoustics and the 'natural characteristics of tones'. He first constructs a new 'scale' suited to both melodic and harmonic purposes. This is derived from an examination of the overtone series and is called Series 1 :

Ex.16

The principal innovations here are that the chromatic as opposed to the diatonic scale now forms the basis of music (all semitones are equally important and the major/minor distinction and its associated concept of 'altered' notes is dispensed with), and that Series 1 presents diminishing degrees of relationship to the first note.

Next he derives a series of intervals, Series 2, from the acoustical phenomenon of combination tones (difference tones). Excepting the octave and the tritone, the intervals are grouped in pairs, thus illustrating his belief that intervals are invertible and have roots (marked with an arrow). Together with his graphic representation of the concept that

[6] *The Craft of Musical Composition* : Book I, Theoretical Part (rev. ed. London, 1945); Book II, Exercises in Two-Part Writing (London, 1941); Book III, Exercises in Three-Part Writing, in preparation (1969), German text. *The Craft of Musical Composition* is a not entirely accurate translation of the German *Unterweisung im Tonsatz*, which means, literally, 'Instruction in the Setting of Notes'. 'Setting of Notes' is broadly analogous to the English 'Harmony and Counterpoint'.

harmonic and melodic strengths pull in opposite directions the series is as follows:

Ex.17

The principal innovations here are that fundamental importance is attached to the individual qualities of intervals and that the idea of absolute consonance and absolute dissonance is rejected: no point divides 'consonance' from 'dissonance'. These two series form the basis of all subsequent arguments.

Chords are combinations of intervals. As such they have roots, determined by the 'best' interval (that nearest the begining of Series 2). Hindemith now constructs a table of six chord-groups,[7] themselves subdivided according to the position of the root, which are 'ranked' according to their interval content as seen in relation to Series 2. Any possible chord may now be accounted for. He then explains that harmonic tension increases as chords move from Group I (triads and inversions), Group II (including major seconds or minor sevenths or both, tritone subordinate), Group III (including seconds or sevenths or both, no tritone) to Group IV (including seconds or sevenths or both, one or more tritones subordinate). In Group V (augmented triads and three-note fourth-chords) and Group VI (diminished triads and diminished sevenths) there is uncertainty and ambiguity. By analysis of chord-group movement, called Harmonic Fluctuation, it is possible to determine the smoothness or otherwise of a progression; of the influence of Series 1 on the chord-root movement, called Degree Progression, the tonal centre (or tonal ambiguity) of a progression and the tonal centres, the modulations, and their relationships in a complete work.[8] Hindemith considered it impossible to escape the influence of tonality, 'a natural force, like gravity'.

The foregoing indicates his principal analytical and compositional tools. Hindemith himself did not consider their use in a complete work

[7] A distinction is made between chords with and without tritones: the tritone 'stamps chords so strongly with its own character that they acquire both something of its indefiniteness and something of its character of motion towards a goal'.

[8] It should be added that in Book 2 of *Traditional Harmony* (London, 1949) he mentions two other concepts, that of 'Tonal Amplitude' (the tension between the tonic chord and each of the other chords in a tonal area seen in relation to Series 1) and 'Harmonic Density' (the rapidity with which harmonies succeed one another).

36

on the grounds that 'exact statement of the principles of tonal organization is outside the bounds of theoretical discussion'; but a simplified plan of the tonal centres in the *Mathis* Symphony will go some way towards illustrating how the relationships of Series 1 can influence large-scale design and contribute towards the recreation of sonata form.

Ex.18

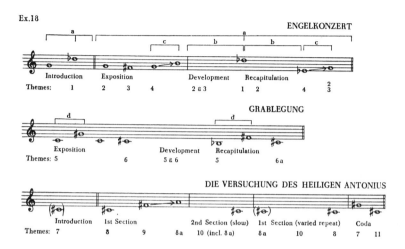

In the introduction to the first movement, a correlation between G and D flat is presented as the structural thesis. This, the most distant possible tonal relationship, is, however, stated rather than argued, and in the main allegro the process of juxtaposing distant tonalities continues (which accounts for the rapt, almost disembodied nature of the movement). In spite of the symmetry between the subsidiary relationships, the final G is precariously balanced. The only really purposeful harmonic movement occurs at the end of the exposition and the recapitulation—to fairly closely related tonalities (four steps away in a Series 1 beginning on G). The slow movement begins from a near relative of G and eventually establishes C sharp (D flat) by cogently argued progressions. Having reached his goal, Hindemith stays there: this tonality dominates the finale.

On a smaller scale, the following analysis of the closing bars of 'Grablegung' explains how harmonic tension is sustained, intensified, and relaxed at the end by a tight control of chord progression. It also shows how the C sharp tonality is stated, diffused, and restated in an appropriately 'mild' cadence by an equally deliberate use of the tonal relationships created by root progressions.

Ex.19

The principal theme of each movement will provide characteristic instances of the relationship between Series 2 and the intervallic content of thematic material. Each begins firmly on the root or fifth of its respective tonic, with 'harmonic' intervals of fifths and fourths, which then give way to the 'melodic' intervals of thirds and seconds.

Ex.20

38

Clearly the tenets of *The Craft of Musical Composition* exerted a powerful influence on the structure and tonal language of the 'Mathis' Symphony. It is important however to realize that the book provides compositional means only, and limited ones at that. There is a popular impression that the remarkable stylistic uniformity of Hindemith's post-*Mathis* music is the result of an imagination desiccated in the prison of a system, or of an arrogant complacency following the discovery of the 'right' path (to paraphrase two critical commonplaces). The magisterial authority of the Symphony is already a warning to the commentator who would find an unhealthy link between Hindemith the theorist and Hindemith the composer, and cite the failings of the one as evidence of the supposed failings of the other.

A musical style is not formed exclusively by the use of certain techniques; and many features of Hindemith's later music are not connected with the theory at all. While the mental discipline imposed by writing the book may have increased his awareness of his identity as a composer or may simply have coincided with this process of self-discovery, it is that identity, that artistic purpose, which is finally responsible for the character of his later music. A review of what may be called the second period of his maturity must therefore take account of the creative personality behind it as well as include a tolerably complete description of its technical features.

In this context, the book itself can be judged a rationale, partly 'scientific', partly intuitive, of certain aspects of his composing process. The 'scientific' element has attracted the wider attention: theories drawn from the 'immutable' laws of Nature will naturally seem to have the ring of truth about them, especially to those who seek a repudiation of atonality and twelve-note music ('which in its avoidance of anything approaching a triad seems to fly in the face of Nature'). Hindemith emphasized this element himself, believing his Series 1 and 2 to embrace discoveries of almost divine provenance. Until the end of his life he considered music which failed to take account of them to be little short of a betrayal. Even the music he wrote himself between 1924 and 1929 is implicitly rejected in the appendix to the first German edition. The book's debt to his instincts as a composer is, however, of greater consequence. If it suited his purpose he turned a blind eye to Nature (his disregard of the seventh harmonic when deriving Series 1 is a case in point). Passages of careful reasoning may be followed by dogmatic assertions without warning and without substantiation (why the three-note fourth-chord should belong to Group V, for example, is not explained). He fails to reconcile his theory that chords can be interpreted in one way only with his acceptance of melodic 'non-chord' notes. And in any case he addressed his subject from the restricted, if broadly-based standpoint of one nurtured in the Austro-German tradition. This degree of subjectivity is the book's strength, and few musicians would expect otherwise from the work of a major composer. It is certainly enough to insure against recent criticism that the acoustical foundations are shaky.[9] It does put an end, however, to Hindemith's evident hopes for providing the grammar for a twentieth-century lingua franca. As a teaching aid *The Craft of Musical Composition* is of limited value, and no blueprint for composition as such. It takes scant account of such matters as counterpoint, form, texture, instrumental colour (in *Traditional Harmony* he advocates the use of the harmonium to test out exercises in 'undeceptive nudity'), rhythm, or tempo, and the exercises are geared to Hindemith's own style—*pace* his contention that the book teaches technique, as opposed to style. Its principal and very considerable claim to attention lies in the means it provides for functional harmonic progression within a language of expanded tonality, and in its insistence on the characteristics of intervals.

In 1948 Hindemith published a revised version of *Das Marienleben*, which includes a lengthy preface discussing his reasons for undertaking the revision, and the musical techniques involved. This preface also implicitly constitutes some kind of artistic confession, and it contains one remark particularly relevant to our purposes. 'I began to glimpse the ideal of a noble music, as near perfect as possible, that I should one day be able to realize.' 'A noble music' is not easy to define, but its overtones of serenity, of acceptance of the natural order of things, of aspiration towards the highest artistic purpose, explain the reasons for the calm at the centre of his post-*Mathis* music, the quality which distinguishes it most readily from the often tense and agitated music of the 1920s, and, for that matter, from the music of the majority of his contemporaries. In striving to deepen the spiritual qualities of an art which, as he saw it, could debase as well as uplift, he was conscious of the moral responsibility demanded of him. This in turn demanded the utmost in technical control, a rejection of music as an outlet for personal expression and its affirmation as a source of social value. His music therefore does not give the impression that it could take on a life of its own; one always senses the guiding hand of the composer. While it can

[9] Hindemith's procedure has been criticized as both tendentious and incorrect. See Norman Cazden, 'Hindemith and Nature', *Music Review*, November 1954; Victor Landau, 'Hindemith the System Builder', *Music Review*, May 1963, and Richard Bobbitt, 'Hindemith's Twelve-tone Scale', *Music Review*, May 1965.

frequently and justifiably be described as expressive, one applies the term to a precisely defined mood analogous to that of the baroque *Affekt*, rather than the highly charged emotional utterance which abruptly changes course or lingers on the unexpected moment. Hindemith aimed to re-create the essence of what he considered the lasting values of music, asking of his listener that he become an active participant in fulfilling music's function of revealing some experience of 'divine order'. In brief his artistic purpose was of restatement, rejuvenation, preservation.

It has been necessary to give a comparatively detailed account of Hindemith's earlier music in order to keep track of the diffusion of interests it represents and to trace the course of an evolving musical language. But from *Mathis der Maler* onwards there was little further 'development', in the accepted sense of the term. For this reason his remaining output can be considered as a single unit, and the chronological approach adopted thus far largely abandoned.

As a superscription to the last movement of the Sonata for Alto Horn and Piano, he wrote:

> Your task is, amid confusion, rush and noise,
> to grasp the lasting, calm, and meaningful,
> and finding it anew, to hold and treasure it.

His later output all proceeds from this profoundly conservative temperament. He wrote for conventional resources and traditional genres, an interpretation of his responsibilities directed towards comprehensibility and usefulness. Perhaps the most striking evidence of this is the huge series of instrumental sonatas compiled between 1935 and 1955 which caters for every common instrument (with the exception of piccolo, bass clarinet, and double bassoon). Although the only moderate technical difficulty of the first, the Sonata for Violin and Piano in E, was considerably increased in some of the subsequent sonatas, their 'for gifted amateurs' cachet remained fundamental. Further evidence is shown by the fact that five symphonies followed the *Mathis* Symphony, nine concertos, numerous chamber pieces—an almost encyclopedic body of works all familiar in their terms of reference. This conservative approach also provided the setting in which he could project his vision of the timelessness of musical experience, in which there could be a synthesis of the baroque and the romantic, the medieval and the modern. Thus his first 'pure' symphony, the Symphony in E flat (1940), absorbs the closed forms of the baroque and the grand Brucknerian paragraphs of the nineteenth century within its highly individual re-creation of the symphonic idea; and while the Organ Concerto of 1962 is characteristic of the often astringent harmonic idiom and the often delicately sensuous orchestration of his last works, it also includes variations on 'Veni Creator Spiritus' and a quotation of 'L'homme armé'.

For Hindemith it was axiomatic that music should be built on the imperishable support of lyric (as opposed to dramatic) melodic line. His later music is nothing if not melodic. The following example of the principal type illustrates his adherence to the traditional sentence-structure of four phrases, with usually a sequential repeat in the second or third and a climax in the last.

Ex.21

Sehr langsam
Str.+Cls.

NOBILISSIMA VISIONE

Though it might be obscured by skilful variation of phrase-length or become part of a larger melodic group (both of which factors apply in the example), this structure remained a fundamental mode of thought, even in melodic material not overtly lyrical. The tendency to form a self-contained unit is very pronounced and accounts for the characteristically deliberate yet unhurried and flowing movement. Such melodies are supported by a firm bass line (often, as in the example, derived from the chaconne bass) and are complemented by harmonies consisting in the main of the typically Hindemithian chords of Group III. With their preponderance of diatonic intervals these create a mildly dissonant harmonic norm, drained of the intense subjective feeling associated with chromatic appoggiaturas. This procedure also leaves room, if necessary, for the more tense chords of Group IV at climaxes and for cadential harmonies in which each part moves with staunch melodic logic to the resolution of triads or bare fifths. Hindemith's restoration of the triad to a position of central harmonic importance, in a language neither artificial nor nostalgic, is in many ways the most characteristic product of his artistic temperament.

A second type comprises more succinct, open-ended melodic ideas of only one or two phrases. Here the need to expand, to 'complete' the implied structure, is appropriate for sonata movements and forms based on the cumulative effect of melodic repetition, such as passacaglias and fugues. They are often concluded with a tailpiece, like the codetta of a fugue subject.

Ex.22 (a)
(Allegro moderato)
Solo

CELLO CONCERTO: first movement
Codetta

(b) (Slow)

LUDUS TONALIS: Fugue 1

The facility with which Hindemith extended his material by imitative techniques, or added poised but expendable countermelodies (regular countersubjects are rare, even in his fugues), again underlines the primacy of the melodic impulse.

As if to compensate for the predominance of these melodic categories, Hindemith also evolved an idiosyncratic form of instrumental recitative in which contours, rhythm, and grouping correspond precisely with an underlying verbal text. An extended use of this procedure can be found in the ballet *Hérodiade* (1944), in which every syllable of the Mallarmé poem which forms the scenario finds its place in the music. Further examples can be found in the Harp Sonata, the Sonata for Two Pianos, and the Horn Concerto.

An obvious consequence of this emphasis on line and structure is that his instrumentation is designed primarily to clarify the line and only in the broadest terms is an expressive means in its own right—which is why by far the most gifted and versatile instrumentalist among twentieth-century composers was the least adventurous of orchestrators and not at his happiest with a non-sustaining instrument such as the piano.

Hindemith placed so high a premium on melody and possessed such remarkable technical facility that what on occasion seems a mechanical reliance on one or other category may give rise to abstractions rather than heard sound images. Expressive content may be squeezed out by the impersonal fifths and fourths or be dissipated by a gesture that is purely formal (Ex. 23, bracket).

Ex.23   STRING QUARTET No. 5

Despite occasional failings of the aural imagination it would be wrong to dismiss such works as the quartet in the above example on this account.

The concept of an unspotted masterpiece is a pernicious one. Any assessment must recognize that a Hindemith work makes its effect as a whole rather than in detail and that incidental blemishes have a marginal effect when set against the strength of the complete design. Hindemith's sense of musical architecture was perhaps the most highly developed of all his musical faculties. On the rare occasions when his formal structures seem to totter (as in the Organ Sonata no. 2, for example, which ends in the wrong key) the listener's discomfort is acute because so unexpected.

Hindemith's preoccupation with the balanced formal design reflects both his quasi-metaphysical view of proportion and the melodic criteria already discussed. His formal procedures may be classified by relating them to the two principal melodic types, the self-contained/static and the incomplete/cumulative. Forms deriving from the first melodic type include numerous adaptations of the cantus firmus principle: thus, for example, the chorale prelude on a Beethoven military march in the second movement of the *Symphonia Serena* and a form built from six varied repetitions of his own melody in the first movement of the Pittsburgh Symphony. The theme and variations also comes in this category. It is significant that in his largest work in this form, *The Four Temperaments* for piano and strings, the proportions and melodic contours of the 'theme' (three themes in this case) are preserved almost literally, and the variations themselves are of a primarily textural and rhythmic nature. Ternary and other arch forms are included here, along with the more individual though no less characteristic forms created by juxtaposing two apparently incompatible melodies and then combining them: this a device of virtuoso appeal in which the listener is afforded the uncommon pleasure of hearing the composer solve the problem he has set himself. The second movement of the Cello Concerto, comprising a serene melody and a rapid dance, is constructed in this way. Further examples may be found in the Horn Sonata, the Quartet no. 6, the *Symphonia Serena*, the Symphony for Concert Band and the Symphony *Die Harmonie der Welt*.

The second category is of forms not deriving from the repetition and arrangement of completed units. This consists, apart from fugues and passacaglias, largely of variations on the sonata idea, and involves more sophisticated harmonic methods. Hindemith's sonata movements are distinguished by the absence of dramatic conflict between thematic material, a feature which often leads to the superposition of first and second subject material, even in expositions, focuses attention on the themes *qua* music as opposed to dramatic gesture and allows the harmonic control to be perceived more readily. In the unassuming first movement of the Sonata for Flute and Piano, for example, the carefully prepared tonal organization (Ex. 24a) tightens the potentially weak relationship between B flat and A, while at the same time foreshadowing the reconciliation of the tonalities and themes in the coda; this final section also completes the 'incomplete' (only two-phrase) structure of the first subject (Ex. 24b).

Ex.24

The first movement of the Symphony in E flat provides an example of Hindemith's method in a less orthodox structure. Here the energy of the ritornello theme is contained in a harmonic framework which both satisfies the need for balance and gives the theme room to develop. Each of the italicized letters in the following tonal diagram is a melodic variant of the ritornello.

Ex.25

This structure, based on a combination of ritornello and sonata forms, reveals the greatest tonal distance from the home tonic in the second (quasi-development) section, and a recapitulation which begins to restore the home area by returning melodically to the first section and absorbing the D flat of that section in a final clinching sequence of tonal areas.

Although these two categories overlap in various respects, the methods involved are distinct enough to render the overriding common purpose that much more dominant. Hindemith never wavered from the view that a piece of music should lead purposefully past any beguiling side roads to a preordained conclusion.

The features summarized above are so pronounced that it would seem possible to build up a picture of the 'average' Hindemith work with a degree of accuracy. But the concluding brief notes on some of his representative later works will show that while the ubiquitous Hindemithian fingerprints are rarely absent, his extraordinarily fertile formal imagination makes the idea of an 'average' work a fiction.

The major work of the years immediately following *Mathis* is the ballet *Nobilissima Visione* (1938). This is a diatonic counterpart to the opera. Its scenario shows many points in common, such as the scene in which St. Francis's illusions of the heroic military life are shattered and he experiences the vision of poverty, selflessness, and neighbourly love which changes his life. There is also a quasi folk-song content ('Ce fut en Mai' by the trouvère Moniot d'Arras, associated with Francis's early life). The ballet lacks obvious box-office appeal, but in the concert suite he assembled later Hindemith rescued some of his most sustained melodic inventions. Extended paragraphs are built up by taking an initial four-phrase unit as the first of a larger unit. Ex. 21, from the first movement, shows such an initial unit. The following transciption, from the second movement, shows a larger grouping. It also illustrates his rhythmic method. Rhythmic novelty in his music is usually by way of counterpoint of tempi. The transcription is in the heard rhythms which operate against the notated pulse of 2/2. (See Ex. 26 on following page.)

As a whole the *Nobilissima Visione* suite epitomizes the essential seriousness and integrity of Hindemith's music. It does not make a frontal assault on the listener's responses, but delves deep into areas of experience that are familiar but unfathomable. If it ultimately leaves a feeling of sadness, this is the sadness, let us say, of falling rain, of a natural phenomenon beyond the realms of personal sentiment.

The exhilarating Cello Concerto (1940), surely one of the finest works of its kind, presents a different aspect of his creative temperament. It is a concerto in the grand manner. Hindemith's individuality is especially apparent in such a work, which offers all the expected ingredients of a post-Mozartian concerto (virtuoso soloist, orchestral tuttis in the right place, solo cadenza followed by trills, thematic prodigality in the finale) as well as a generous allowance of special

Ex.26

features (the fascinating design of the second movement already mentioned, and the 'twittering machine' instrumentation in the finale) and yet which leaves the commentator at a loss to draw any really relevant comparison with an earlier model. Hindemith follows the tradition, rather than any isolated product of it. His particular contribution is to emphasize the partnership between solo and orchestra, playing down the element of competition. This is made clear at the beginning when the cantabile second theme of the first group (Ex. 22a) is no sooner stated than combined with the alert and rhythmic first theme.

Perhaps the extreme instance of Hindemith's almost geometrical approach to form is *Ludus Tonalis* for piano (1942). This work consists of twelve carefully contrasted three-part fugues (he held that the ear could distinguish no more than three parts), linked by interludes, which branch out from C to F sharp in the order of Series 1: a scheme which provides the complete range of tonalities and, in Hindemith's terms, a demonstration of systematic weakening of tonal orientation. This built-in unity is reinforced by framing the whole with a Praeludium and a Postludium which are mirror inversions of each other, and by applying the mirror technique itself on a large scale. There are marked thematic correspondences between the central fugues and interludes, which become more tenuous as one works outwards: and there are analogous structural relationships.

Ex. 27

Praeludium	Postludium
Fugue 1 (Triple fugue)	Fugue 12 (Binary form)
Fugue 2 (Stretto fugue)	Fugue 11 (Canon)
Fugue 3 (Repeat by retrograde)	Fugue 10 (Repeat by inversion)
Fugue 4 (Double fugue)	Fugue 9 (Combination by inversion, retrograde, etc.)
Fugue 5 (a a b form)	Fugue 8 (a a b form)
Fugue 6 (Arch form)	Fugue 7 (Arch form)

This symmetry is, in fact, oddly disturbed, since while the postlude leads the tonality back from F sharp to C, the prelude takes it from C to an F sharp which is then left high and dry. But didactic and architectural purposes are in any case pushed aside by the sheer eloquence of the music, which obliges the listener constantly to readjust his tonal sights. *Ludus Tonalis* encompasses the whole range of Hindemith's expressive resource at that time, from the steely logic of the part-writing in Fugue 4 to the tragic beauty of Fugue 12.

Ex.28

Fugue 4
(With energy)

Fugue 12
Very quiet

The most extrovert work Hindemith wrote is the *Symphonic Metamorphoses on Themes by Carl Maria von Weber* (1943), quite the reverse of what might be expected from the portentous title. It is a brilliant orchestral showpiece couched in a language unmistakably his own, but close enough to the originals to register immediately with a wide audience. Weber is treated neither with reverence nor with condescension. While the harmonies and textures of the unpretentious models[10] are radically altered, Hindemith keeps very close to their content and shape, parting company only in the riotous coda to the finale and in the colourful scherzo.

In the preface to the 1948 revision of *Das Marienleben*, the 1923 version is severely criticized for its awkward voice part, its empirical harmony, its formlessness. This is already an instance of unusual candour for a creative artist, even if the musical language of the revision contains no surprises to the listener acquainted with Hindemith's post-*Mathis* style. For the new version, fourteen of the fifteen songs are altered in some degree, the cycle is organized into clear tonal groups, and dynamic and expressive intensity is carefully controlled (heard to best advantage in the marvellously sustained lead from the climactic

Ex.29
Ruhige Viertel

[10] No. 4 from *8 Stücke*, op. 60; no. 2 from *Six Pièces Faciles*, op. 3; no. 2 and no. 7 from the *8 Stücke* (all for piano duet) for the first, third, and fourth movements. The second movement is based on a motive Weber found in Rousseau's music dictionary under Chinese music and used in his *Turandot* music.

'Von der Hochzeit zu Kana' to the two songs of the Passion). But the most intriguing aspect of the revision concerns the conceptual symbolism attributed to the relationships of Series 1. E, for example, the tonal centre of the work, represents 'the nature of Mary's Son'. The theme from 'Vom Tode Maria', a theme and variations, will illustrate the extent of Hindemith's procedure (Ex. 29). The commentary is his own. 'We are made aware of the entrance into infinity (C, bar 1), which, with its utter inexorability (C sharp, 2–3), but yet with its infinite gentleness (diffuse G, 4), fills us with a feeling of our own minuteness (F sharp, 5–6). Although we trust fate (D, 7), we are none the less troubled by a slight feeling of lack of understanding (B flat, 8). The believer will recognize in the Redeemer (E, 9–10) and in his once earthly mother (B, 11) his guides toward the final purity of death (E flat, 11–12).' Whether or not the listener can endorse these interpretations, their systematic use adds an associative meaning and a structural coherence to the work which, together with the serenity of the tonal language, imparts a grandeur absent from the original version.

The revision of *Das Marienleben* is a work of quite different substance from the original. To speak of 'improvement' seems irrelevant. Whether this can be said of the revisions of *Cardillac* (1952) and *Neues vom Tage* (1953) is less certain. In *Cardillac*, for which Hindemith himself wrote an entirely new text, the introduction of more conventional human relationships, a visions scene after the manner of *Mathis*, and a new and rather obviously 'theatrical' act (an opera within an opera —the symbolically apposite enactment of a section from Lully's *Phaeton*) certainly make for more comprehensible dramatic events and smoother transitions. But this, together with the retention of much of the original music (often overlaid with new vocal lines), weakens the directness and bite of the original, which willy-nilly evoked the moral questions which are somewhat ingenuously spelt out at the end of the revision. Much the same could be said of *Neues vom Tage*, whose ending now permits Laura and Edward to escape with their privacy.

The central work of Hindemith's last years is the opera *Die Harmonie der Welt* (The Harmony of the World), which was completed in 1957, but which had occupied him on and off for several years. On one level this huge work is the culmination of a process in which Hindemith's preoccupation with the theme of the artist is taken from the craftsman (Cardillac), to the creative genius (Mathis) and finally to the visionary philosopher, Johannes Kepler; on another, it is the most comprehensive expression of his artistic credo. Kepler (1571–1630) was a typical product of the Renaissance, at once mathematician, musician, astronomer, and philosopher. He had an almost obsessional belief in *musica mundana*, the music of the spheres—the idea that divine revelation is present in a 'harmony' of the solar system, which harmony can be expressed in musical terms. By relating the mathematical proportions underlying the structure of sound to the orbits of the planets round the sun, he ultimately proposed[11] the actual sounds made by the planets individually and collectively. Kepler believed he had unlocked the secrets of *musica mundana*. Hindemith believed (if one may so interpret a rather obscure passage in *The Craft of Musical Composition*)[12] that by revealing proportional relationships within the 'atom' of the single note, as set out in Series 1 and 2, he had gone further and discovered laws which were common to *musica mundana* and the other two ancient musical concepts, *musica humana* (the 'music' sounding between two human souls—as in love) and *musica instrumentalis* (that produced on instruments or voices). In short he believed that the element of divine revelation was not confined to the music of the spheres. It can be present in music as we know it. In the opera he used Kepler's life to dramatize this visionary idea.

The ultimate effect of the opera is of one gigantic upbeat to the crucial last scene which attempts an allegorical representation of the Harmony of the World. The means used to achieve this are extremely complex in detail, but simple in the basic premise of suppressing development of character or situation until the final scene. There is no plot in the conventional sense of the word. Isolated episodes from Kepler's life follow chronologically, but without dramatic inevitability.[13] A pageant of historical personages is built up, ranging from those whose actions frustrate Kepler's work (the two Emperors, Rudolf II and Ferdinand II, the General Wallenstein and Kepler's mother Katharina, who was tried for witchcraft) to those who provide comfort and encouragement (his second wife Susanna and his little daughter Susanna). Kepler himself, although buffeted by circumstance, remains the intractable bearer of his mystic vision. None of the characters fits into a composite dramatic scheme until the final scene, in which each takes his

[11] The book in which his ideas were most fully developed is *Harmonice Mundi*, the Harmony of the World.

[12] See pp. 53-4.

[13] In the companion Symphony *Die Harmonie der Welt* these episodic dramatic events are converted into a carefully controlled structure in which the tension of the first movement is gradually released in the second and resolved in the third, the passacaglia of the last scene. This is the only substantial quotation from the opera. The other movements contain reworkings of material drawn from the whole work.

place as one of the members of the Harmony of the World.[14] This is the fulfilment of Kepler's vision, which he can experience only after death.

Musically the opera reflects in key relationships and intervallic shapes (geared to the two Series) Kepler's distance from this fulfilment. The key of the final scene, a massive passacaglia, is E (significantly, also the tonal centre of *Das Marienleben*). Until this point the keys swing in directions nearer or further from this centre according to the character of the scenes. The key of the trial scene is thus B flat, that of Susanna's bridal song A. With Kepler's death the final E is reached. In the passacaglia Hindemith is, of course, not presuming to create a real symbol of the postulated harmony. He progresses towards it. The final E major triad is in this context far more than a conventional major key ending. Hindemith's attitude towards the major triad had clearly developed from one, in *The Craft of Musical Composition*, of simple acceptance (of its natural and inevitable qualities) to one, in the opera, almost of humility. The real Harmony begins after the major triad.

In this sense *Die Harmonie der Welt* is concerned with ontological notions of the infinite, with a world of no beginnings and no ends, and a tiny aspect of this is developed in his last opera, *The Long Christmas Dinner* (1960), written to a text by Thornton Wilder. This little parable of the unending cycles of birth and death is presented as a family scene, generations succeeding one another, the small talk going on from one Christmas to the next, and the opera ending with the promise of a new sequence of events exactly as before. Hindemith's score contains some of his most tender and translucent music, including a sextet of almost Schubertian delicacy harmonized exclusively in triads.

Hindemith's new feeling for the triad led to many similar sections in his last works and a changed approach to harmony as such. With it came a keener appreciation of sound, as opposed to harmonic structure. Trends in this direction were perceptible in the Cello Sonata of 1948 and the Double Bass Sonata of the following year, which, although predominantly light and capricious, contains a recitativo variation with markedly astringent harmonies. The last of the sonatas, the Tuba Sonata, has an even more 'dissonant' variation including twelve-note chords deriving from a twelve-note theme. *Die Harmonie der Welt* itself is rich in chords of Group IV and many passages in the last works suggest that having made so complete an artistic statement in the opera Hindemith now felt the need to branch out afresh. Certainly the dense chordal groupings in the following characteristic excerpt, the beginning of the finale of the Pittsburgh Symphony, demonstrate that the principles

[14] In this connection see p. 57 of *The Craft of Musical Composition*.

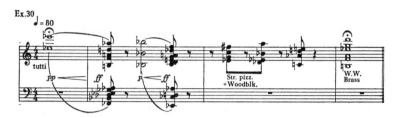

of smooth harmonic rise and fall associated with *The Craft of Musical Composition* are, at least in the smaller context, being adapted to an approach which also admits timbre as a structural element. This new sensitivity to timbre, especially evident in the prismatic orchestral textures of the Organ Concerto, contrasts sharply with the efficient but often colourless orchestral style of the 30s and 40s. There is another contrast in thematic treatment. Such features as the eight-note pattern

of uncharacterized pitches serving as basic material for the variations of the Pittsburgh Symphony finale, and the almost serial three-note motive of the opening section from one of the Motets for voice and piano (thirteen settings from the Gospels) (Ex. 31 on previous page) tempt one to suppose that, like Stravinsky, Hindemith might eventually have come to terms with Schoenbergian methods. But at the same time he retained his allegiance to the balanced melodic paragraph, and was still able, as in the final bars of his last work, the Mass for unaccompanied chorus, to draw poignant beauty from a triadic tonal language. Such ambiguity is part of the distinctive character of the last works. Their essentially introspective flavour makes it plain that had he attempted to include serialism in his conception of the totality of musical experience he would have fought a losing battle with his better self. Although he may secretly have come to regret his conservatism, it was inescapable.

Hindemith's current reputation is at a low ebb, and this principally because this conservatism is at odds with contemporary musical values. His music lacks that element of the irrational, the 'divine madness' evidently a *sine qua non* for the creative artist of the mid-twentieth century; and if greatness is equated with a capacity to stimulate later styles, Hindemith's negligible influence on younger composers can be regarded as another nail in his coffin. He began to part company with the spirit of the times in the 1940s. Thereafter he lost touch so completely that his music can already be seen with some detachment as belonging to a past era. In this respect particular stylistic features and leanings towards mysticism show him to be not only a typically German composer who re-created his heritage in twentieth-century terms, but also one who added to his heritage with a synthesis of many aspects of it; so that he emerges as the last great bearer of a tradition stretching back, through Strauss and Brahms, to the days of the early baroque.

But Hindemith cannot be considered solely in national terms, nor was he always an isolated figure. His discovery of German folk-music was one of the most important single events in his life; this was true also of Stravinsky, Bartók, Vaughan Williams, and many other composers who found their creative identity in folk-music. Hindemith indeed was a typically twentieth-century as well as a typically German composer, typical in his neo-classicism (both the rigidly objective neo-classicism of, for example, the *Kammermusik* series and Stravinsky's Piano Concerto, and its less formalized and more documentary aspects as in *Neues vom Tage* and Schoenberg's *Von Heute auf Morgen*) and in his return to classical sonata forms at a time when Bartók, Schoenberg and Stravinsky were finding a similar need for retrenchment. Though not strictly comparable to Schoenberg's twelve-note method or Messiaen's *Technique de mon langage musical*, *The Craft of Musical Composition* is representative with these other methods of a general desire to impose order on a potentially chaotic situation. What makes him a key figure in twentieth-century music is, firstly, his championship of amateur music. It is difficult to imagine how this field of activity would have developed if a composer of Hindemith's stature had not set the pace. Of greater significance is his championship of a tonal harmonic language. This occurred when he was widely regarded as a major, if not the central figure of his time, and Hindemith's authority undoubtedly helped to create a climate in which a second generation of twentieth-century composers could confidently draw new life from that language.

Hindemith's work as a teacher and practising musician is further confirmation of a position in the centre of twentieth-century music. Little can be gained from asking why he did not maintain that position, or whether he might have maintained it had he not written *The Craft of Musical Composition*. Some old men have been explorers, some not. Most composers feel the need to work within limits, within some conception of an ordered truth, and Hindemith is exceptional only in that his order was made public. It was obviously a stimulus to his creative imagination, otherwise a man of his intelligence would not have defended it both in music and words with such zeal, and it was also dangerously superficial, otherwise he would have published its third part. Hindemith's conservatism was inborn. Like Bach, he was considered an antiquated irrelevance during his lifetime. But his masterly music remains, and there is no reason to suppose that the composer of the *Kammermusik* and *Konzertmusik* series, of *Cardillac* and *Mathis der Maler*, of the Cello Concerto and the Organ Concerto, will remain a peripheral figure for long. Hindemith was obviously a lesser figure than Stravinsky or Schoenberg, a greater one than Milhaud or Prokofiev—but it is invidious and misleading to make comparisons. He had more in common with Braque than any musical contemporary. In the words of Patrick Heron,[15] Braque reminds a contemporary audience, 'fed to satiety on brilliant innovation, frenzied novelty and every variety of spontaneous expression, that, after all, permanence, grandeur, deliberation, lucidity and calm are paramount virtues of the art of painting.' This could as well have been said of Hindemith.

[15] *The Changing Forms of Art* (London, 1955), p. 81.

LIST OF HINDEMITH'S
PRINCIPAL WORKS

OPERAS

Mörder, Hoffnung der Frauen, op. 12 (1919)—*Das Nusch-Nuschi*, op. 20 (1920)—*Sancta Susanna*, op. 21 (1921)—*Cardillac*, op. 39 (1926), revised version (1952)—*Hin und Zurück*, op. 45a (1927)—*Neues vom Tage* (1929), revised version (1953)—*Lehrstück* (1929)—*Wir bauen eine Stadt* (1930)—*Mathis der Maler* (1934–5)—*Die Harmonie der Welt* (1956–7)—*The Long Christmas Dinner* (1960)

BALLETS

Der Dämon, op. 28 (1922)—*Nobilissima Visione* (1938)—*The Four Temperaments* (1940)—*Hérodiade* (1944)

CHORAL WORKS WITH ORCHESTRA

Das Unaufhörliche (1930)—*When Lilacs Last in the Door-yard Bloom'd*, A Requiem 'for those we love' (1946)—*Apparebit repentina dies*, for chorus and brass (1947)—*Ite, angeli veloces* (1953–5)

ORCHESTRAL WORKS AND CONCERTOS

Kammermusik No. 1, op. 24, No. 1 (1921) for chamber orchestra—*Kammermusik No. 2* (Piano Concerto), op. 36, No. 1 (1924)—*Kammermusik No. 3* (Cello Concerto), op. 36, No. 2 (1925)—*Kammermusik No. 4* (Violin Concerto), op. 36, No. 3 (1925)—*Concerto for Orchestra*, op. 38 (1925)—*Konzertmusik for Wind*, op. 41 (1926)—*Kammermusik No. 5* (Viola Concerto), op. 36, No. 4 (1927)—*Kammermusik No. 6* (Viola d'amore Concerto), op. 45, No. 1 (1927)—*Kammermusik No. 7* (Organ Concerto), op. 46, No. 2 (1927)—*Konzertmusik for Viola and Large Chamber Orchestra*, op. 48 (1930)—*Konzertmusik for Piano, Brass and Two Harps*, op. 49 (1930)—*Konzertmusik for Brass and Strings*, op. 50 (1930)—*Philharmonic Concerto* (1932)—*Symphony: Mathis der Maler* (1934)—*Der Schwanendreher*, Concerto for viola and small orchestra (1935)—*Trauermusik* for viola and strings (1936)—*Symphonic Dances* (1937)—Suite *Nobilissima Visione* (1938)—*Violin Concerto* (1939)—*Symphony in E flat* (1940)—*Cello Concerto* (1940)—*Symphonic Metamorphoses on Themes by Carl Maria von Weber* (1943)—*Piano Concerto* (1945)—*Symphonia Serena* (1946)—*Clarinet Concerto* (1947)—*Concerto for Woodwind, Harp and Orchestra* (1949)—*Concerto for Trumpet, Bassoon and Strings* (1949)—*Horn Concerto* (1949)—*Sinfonietta in E* (1949)—*Symphony in B flat for*

Concert Band (1951)—*Symphony: Die Harmonie der Welt* (1951)—*Pittsburgh Symphony* (1958)—*Organ Concerto* (1962)

CHAMBER MUSIC

Quartet No. 1, op. 10 (1918)—*Quartet No. 2*, op. 16 (1921)—*Suite 1922* for piano (1922)—*Quartet No. 3*, op. 22 (1922)—*Kleine Kammermusik* for wind quintet op. 24, No. 2 (1922)—*Clarinet Quintet* (1923)—*Quartet No. 4*, op. 32 (1923)—*String Trio No. 1*, op. 34 (1924)—*Trio* for piano, viola and heckelphone (1928)—*String Trio No. 2* (1933)—*Quartet* for clarinet, violin, cello and piano (1938)—*Ludus Tonalis* for piano (1942)—*Quartet No. 5* in E flat (1943) —*Quartet No. 6* in E flat (1945)—*Septet* for wind quintet, bass clarinet and trumpet (1948)—*Sonata for Four Horns* (1952)—*Octet* for clarinet, horn, bassoon, violin, two violas, cello and double bass (1957–8)
Solo Sonatas with piano (unless otherwise stated):
for Violin in E flat, op. 11, No. 1 (1918), in D, op. 11, No. 2 (1918), op. 31, No. 1 (solo) and No. 2 (solo) (1924), in E (1935), in C (1939)—for Viola in F, op. 11, No. 4 (1919), op. 11, No. 5 (solo) (1919), op. 25, No. 1 (1922), in C (1939)—for Viola d'amore op. 25, No. 2 (1923)—for Cello, op. 11, No. 3 (1919), op. 25, No. 3 (solo) (1923), (1948)—for Double Bass (1949)—for Flute (1936)—for Oboe (1938)—for Cor Anglais (1941)—for Clarinet (1939) —for Bassoon (1938)—for Horn (1939)—for Alto Horn (or horn, or saxophone) (1943)—for Trumpet (1939)—for Trombone (1941)—for Tuba (1955) —for Piano No. 1 (1936), No. 2 (1936), No. 3 (1936)—for Piano Duet (1938) —for Two Pianos (1942)—for Organ No. 1 (1937), No. 2 (1937), No. 3 (1940)—for Harp (1939)

VOCAL AND CHORAL WORKS

Das Marienleben for soprano and piano (1923), revised version (1948)—*Lieder nach alten Texten* (1923), revised version *Five Songs on Old Texts* for unaccompanied chorus (1936)—*Six Chansons* for unaccompanied chorus (1939) —Thirteen *Motets* for soprano or tenor and piano (1941–60)—Twelve *Madrigals* for unaccompanied chorus (1958)—Mass (1963)

A complete list of Hindemith's published music is issued by Schott. A chronological list of published and unpublished music is included in *Paul Hindemith: Zeugnis in Bildern* (Mainz, 1961) and *Paul Hindemith: Die letzten Jahren* (Mainz, 1965), both 'picture' biographies.

REFERENCES

The only published books devoted exclusively to Hindemith are (apart from those mentioned in the list above) Heinrich Strobel, *Paul Hindemith*, 3rd ed. (Mainz, 1948) and Hans Ludwig Schilling, *Paul Hindemith's Cardillac* (Würzburg, 1962). Useful articles can be found in *Die Musik in Geschichte und Gegenwart* (Kassel, 1949–68), in the *Riemann Musik Lexicon*, ed. Willibald Gurlitt (Mainz, 1959) and *Cobbett's Cyclopedic Survey of Chamber Music* 2nd ed., ed. Colin Mason (London, 1963). Other articles are listed in Elizabeth Westphal's *Paul Hindemith: Eine Bibliographie des In- und Auslandes seit 1922* (Cologne, 1957), which was continued in *Paul Hindemith: Emigration und Ruckkehr nach Europa* (the catalogue of an exhibition held at the Frankfurt State and University Library in November and December 1965). Since this monograph was first published, the following important additions to Hindemith literature have appeared: Andres Briner, *Paul Hindemith* (Zürich, 1971) and the *Hindemith-Jahrbuch* 1971/1 (Mainz, 1971).